# ILLUSIONS

## OBSERVING MY REALITY

MELANIE THIEDE

**PROMINENT**
BOOKS

5830 E 2nd St, Ste 7000 #9983
Casper, WY 82609
USA

# CONTENTS

## Section 1:
## POETRY

Section 2:
# SHORT STORIES & JOURNALS

## Section 3:
# SHORT RESEARCH & ESSAYS

## Section 4:
# WORDS OF WISDOM & QUOTES

## Section 5:
# LIFE LESSONS & BLOGS

# PREFACE

There are both emotional explorative poems and concrete poems in the first section, some of which were school assignments. The sections are written in chronological format in each section, starting from poems that were written when I was seven years old up to poems written at 29 years old. . Through many trials and tribulations, school yard incidents, classroom squabbles; I have learned that it is okay to be different and that one should rejoice in our differences. I am now over 40, and I am looking forward to discovering where my life leads me in the next twenty years.

My hope is that my words will help others, and that my experiences may help explain or clarify what you or someone you know may be going through.

# ABOUT THE AUTHOR

*About The Author:* Melanie Laurie Thiede

Being emotionally centered is difficult in our current society in North America. Growing up in Canada as a young lesbian of European descent with a small speech impediment was not easy at times. Through many trials and tribulations, school yard incidents, classroom squabbles; I have learned that it is okay to be different and that one should rejoice in our differences. I am looking forward to discovering where my life leads me in the next twenty years.

# INTRO: ABOUT THE BOOK & AUTHOR

*About The Author:* Melanie Laurie Thiede

Melanie Thiede started life in Montreal, Quebec and attended various public and private schools, until after grade 11. She then moved with her mom and two Yorkies to British Columbia where Melanie attended grade 12 and did her first year of college. Then transferred to Lakehead University where she completed a 3 year bachelors degree with a major in psychology. Then in 2021 she completed an associates of science degree from the University of the People.

Melanie has published a poetry book in 2010 entitled Illusions: My Journey Into Reality and shared her work with others in various media formats including a blog and several online postings of Fan Fiction. Melanie Thiede is a recent university graduate and currently works as an Animal Communicator and Energy Work Practitioner on Vancouver Island and a Virtual Assistant part time.

*About This Book:* Observing My Reality Through Prose

The pieces in this book are arranged when possible in chronological order. The dates on the poems are the years in which the story or poem was originally written and in some cases, when the item was edited or revised. The revisions are mainly correcting for poor word choice, or for explaining what is meant in a clearer way than I had available to me at a younger age. There are both emotional explorative poems and concrete poems here many of which were in my first book, however there are some new additions that were not.

It is my hope that the reader enjoys reading my poems, stories and essays then takes something away with themselves after-wards. As for my book reports, essays and projects, it is my hope here to give you and idea of some of my interests, passions, ideology and thought processes over my schooling years. I welcome feedback or letters from readers both by social media and email which will be provided on the final pages of the book.

Each section of this book is written in a chronological format whenever possible, starting from pieces that were written when I was eight years old up to pieces written at 29 years old. The words of wisdom, yearbook quotes and some of my life lessons include quotes that I have collected from various sources such as my mother's school yearbooks and mine.

Credit is given to those I have found in other sources. The letters, journals and essays have been written for school assignments over the years. Some are just personal diaries that I have written. I have also included a few book reports and book reviews, as I received a few questions from readers about my favorite books. In many cases the assignments have become part of who I am or what I am passionate about and what I feel connected to.

If my readers want to purchase a signed copy of this book or my first one, please email me at illusions1to3@gmail.com and I will tell you how to go about getting a personalized signed copy, and for those who know me personally, you get a discount code by email!

All the best for the future.

Melanie L. Thiede

# DEDICATION

Dedication to my readers and friends of all ages:

This work is one that has taken nearly two decades to create, complete and compile. There were many people who helped me throughout my life so far, to understand and to grow into the wise, caring woman I am today. I wish to thank those with whom I have I have bonded, and have befriended over the years for sticking by me when times were tough, when things were good, and all the in between times.

Teachers have taught me to never give up on my dreams, to reach for the highest star, and that we may sometimes land on a star to the left or right of your chosen star. Many of them inspired me to remain creative, when others wanted me not to be different and write concretely, when that is not in my nature.

I wish to dedicate this compilation of poems, stories and words of wisdom to my parents, my friends and my teachers who have all helped me to become the person I am today.

Thank you to all of you who have helped me grow, inspired me and befriended me.

Melanie Laurie Thiede

# SECTION 1:

# POETRY

# LE PETIT PRINTEMPS

Le petit printemps
Tout vert, tout vert
R'emplace l'hiver
Tout blanc, tout blanc
C'est une moineau
Tout gris, tout gris
Qui me l'a dit?
Qui me l'a dit?

Spring 1987

# WHAT MAKES ME SMILE?

What makes me happy
When I ride my bike outside
When I meet and greet last year's teachers
When mom makes her chop suey.

November 1987

# SPRING

S is for tasting super ice cream
P is for the parks that we go to in the spring
R is for riding my bike to the park
I is for insects who come out in spring
N is for Mother Nature, who cares for our flowers
G is for good times which we will have.

Spring 1988

# SUMMER

S is for sliding down a slide with a friend
U is for umbrellas to use when it rains
M is for marshmallows to eat around the campfire
M is for mother who takes me to the pool.
E is for the excitement that we feel
R is for the roses that bloom in summer.

Summer 1988

# REMEMBRANCE DAY

Remembering the dead
Embrace someone you love
Mourning, what you do after someone dies
Empty your life is when they die
Mornings you're alone
Bidding good-bye!
Rose which we place on the grave
Angry after they die
Nourishment neglected
Caring for loved ones
Exactly the end of this
Dove means peace
Above in Heaven
Yesterday I was okay.

Summer 1988

# GIVING THANKS

I thank thee for the
Trees and the breeze
For the flea and the bee
I thank thee.
For the buds that bloom
For the bed and the broom
Also for the bear and the air
I thank thee.
We dine while sipping wine
Tonight under the stars
Not in the car or in the home
I love thee. I thank thee.

September 1990

# OPINIONS

I like school; I like soccer
I love myself
I'm Me.
Me and Mom; Me and Dad
I don't care
I love both
I'm Me.
Old or young
Your parents may be
They're still yours
I'm Me.

September 1990

# GROWING UP

I used to crawl
I felt like I had to bawl
Now I walk and talk
Speaking in half rhymes
Now uttering in thyme no more.

November 1990

# WORK

When you work
Scrubbing floors, doors
Windows too- it all seems to be the same.
Scrub the shelves down
Tables need to squeak as they
Are cleaned-then it's time to
Recycle the towels I used
Outside I hear the birds sing.

September 1991

# THE PLANETS & OUR SUN

All I need are the planets
Mars, Jupiter, and Mercury
All I need are my friends
Wherever they may be
They are important to me.
Influenced by the sun for growth
Decisions made easier by numbers
Emotions to guide me to the north star
Friendships cultivated with the Earth
They are all important to me.
With the moons swinging by
Picking up the colors of the sea
Alternating control with the sun
Cultivating, growing with each
Passing year, and day
They are important to me.

September 1991 (completed December 2008)

# WHAT IS LOVE?

Love, Love
It's everywhere
But what is love?
Love, care and adore
You can love a partner
You can care for a toy
I like when adore
Is around to play
Love is a heart
That never goes away
If love isn't there
You have not been alive.

Spring 1991

# FRIENDS

Friends can help you
Friends can talk to you
They laugh with you, not at you
They play with you
They are just like me
Friends can read your mind.

September 1991 (In Conjunction with J. McNamara)

# LIFE ISN'T FAIR

You can't always get
Everything that you want
If you have to leave
You've got to do it
Leaving your friends
A half an hour away
Living where you don't do anything
Except watch the television set
When you want to play
You have to telephone
Decide where you want to go
Drive for a while in your vehicle
But life isn't fair
When kids are mean
You can either fight or leave.

Fall 1992

# LOVE IS GREAT

Love is great,
If you have one love in your life
You will be happy; know you are lucky
If your love leaves you
You will miss them; it is okay to cry
You can always find another
There are wonderful people everywhere.

Fall 1992

# L'AMOUR EST MAGNIFIQUE

L'Amour est magnifique
Si tu as une amoureux dans ta vie
Ta vie aurais bonne la restant de ta vie
Si ton amoureux te laisse
Tu vas etre triste
Tu peut trouver une autre.

Fall 1992

# WHAT IS A CLOUD?

A cloud is a thing
That gives us rain
This makes flowers grow
A cloud brings chills
A cloud bring the breeze
I don't know how
The clouds do all of these
We need the clouds
Rain and thunder maybe not
Leave some time for the sun.

Fall 1992

# TRAFFIC

Here we are
At the light
Of an intersection
Wait, wait, wait.
First the light turns Yellow
Then it turns Red
Finally it turns Green
Go, go, go.

September 1992

# WHAT'S CUTE

Cute can be something
That is small in size
Something you like, sometimes you don't
Most of the time you love cute things.

Fall 1992

# DOGS

Dogs are cute and some are big
Dogs are man's best friend
They're great to get to know.

Fall 1992

# WHAT IS LOVE?

Love, Love; It's everywhere
But what is love? Love, care and adore
You can love a partner
You can care for a toy I like when adore
Is around to play
Love is a heart that never goes away
If love isn't there
You have not been alive.

April 1992

# IF YOU LOVE ME
# (THEN TELL ME SO)

If you love me than tell me so
Why must you hide what's inside
Why couldn't you show me?
If you love me then let me see.
You can buy me a diamond ring
You could even sing or even make me king.
If I tell you I hope you will understand
That I love you, and you don't have to make me anything
Because I know you love me too;
So please will you always Keep your smile where I can see
Just how you feel about me.

June 1992

# THE EARTH IS OUR HOME

Earth is our home to keep
We want to live here
The Earth is our home
Each of us should keep it clean
We can do one thing each and it should go along way
To have and to hold, our earth, our home, our world
I am proud to be one of them, the Earthlings as they call us
Each time someone tells a heroic story or shows a picturesque scene
We need to step up to clean it over and over
Pollution is no gift, to the ones left behind.
Each person alive today will be
The recipient of the gift of air, water, soil and such
Protect it from becoming a dump for trash
Keep the world clean for it may be the only home we have.

December 1992

# What Is A Cloud?

A cloud is a thing that gives us rain
A cloud is a thing that brings
Rain, wind and snow
Rain makes flowers grow
A cloud brings chills
A thing of wonder and odd beauty
A cloud brings the breeze I don't know how
The clouds do all of these.
We need the clouds, rain and thunder maybe not
Leave some time for the sun.

November 1992

# A Beach

Cool, dry, peach
Wet, splash, sand
Seashore, wet, dry
Long, wide or narrow
A Beach.

Fall 1992

# STARS

Stars
Twinkle all night
Really Bright.
Stars twinkle all night really bright.

Fall 1992

# PAPA, I WILL

Papa, this is for you
I always loved you and respect your actions
I always will love you, papa.
When you are mad at me too I know I will only have
One True father, and you are mine
I love you, papa.

Spring 1993

# MY LOVE

My love went away
May never come back
I cried many nights
I'll miss her
My love left me
Or did I leave her?
She's gone far away and
May never come back.

May 1993

# WAR 2

War, who likes war?
War is fighting and death
It can change your life.
If a loved one dies you will cry
You'll mourn for them; you may live on.

Spring 1993

# A Sister's Love Survives

What is a sister? you ask
I think I may know but I'm not sure
What is a friend? You ask again
A friend stands by you in all cases, scenarios
How do you know you have a true friend? You observe.
You shape your own life according to your views
Borrow views and opinions of others
Or create your own version with a mixed view
A sister's love can survive the biggest fights
Can survive throughout world wars
Will always exist, no matter what
As we care connected on a spiritual level
We have become inseparable, through time and space
We were always one, and will always be.
I was unsure I would succeed
You stood by me and encouraged me
Little by little I grew
We helped each other past our fears
Grew closer throughout the years.
This is what a sister's love is all about
A Sister's Love Survives.

November 1993

# BICYCLES

Bicycling
Speeding, slowing
Stop, look, going
Think, crossover look, speed up
Car, slowly, faster
Trying, failed- dead.

Spring 1993

# PEARLS

Pearls are bright
Bright, sunlight
Dive, search, seashells
Catch, open, dead, disappointed
Bring and return to air.

Spring 1993

# SI TU ME DONNE

Si tu me donne un bec
Je vais me tenir en garde
Si tu me donne des fleurs
Je vais les mettres dans l'eau.
Si tu me donne l'amour
Je vais te donne l'amour en retour
Si tu me laisse - je pourrai mourir.

Spring 1993

# TRAFFIC

Cars are speeding by Not knowing the speed limit.

Spring 1993

# HAWK

Bird, swooping down from above
Ready to dive; Grabbing a salmon in its talons.

Spring 1993

# SEAWEED

Seaweed, swaying side to side with slime on it
Playground for critters all year long.

Spring 1993

# WHEN I WAS FIVE

Standing in the snow listening to the
Eulogy being given
Family crying all around me
While granddad was interred.
This happened when I was five.
I stood there frozen and unsure
Rules hadn't been explained
Mother was now fatherless
Grandmother was a widow
They both loved him very much
People watched and cried
Standing around a grave
When I was five.
Mom was trembling
How could I help as I was only five?
I went to hold mother
I told her that it was okay to miss him.
All this happened when I was five.

January 1994

# MY CHILD'S WORD

I've travelled far- to many of life's destinations
Looking for answers to all of life's questions
I was amazed at how few I found
I looked in some of the corners of our world
Other people were asking the same questions
And had not found the answers.
When I finally got home
I found that my life was nearly over and not
One of my questions had been answered
When I was on my deathbed
My child told me the answer to my one and only question;
Had I helped anyone?
Had I made a difference?
Her answer was the last thing I heard - YES.

January 1994

# MEMORIES

Lying on the sand
On a deserted beach
Thinking of the past
Remembering the times I spent there
When I was young.
Building sand castles and playing in the sand.
What great memories!

Spring 1994

# ICE CREAM SUNDAE

Here I have a huge cup
Filled with ice cream and other goodies
Strawberry, Chocolate, Vanilla
Yum, Yum, Yum.
First I eat the cherry
Second I eat the whipping cream
Third I eat the sprinkles
Rich, Rich, Rich.
Second to last I eat the chocolate syrup
Fifth I eat what I've been waiting for
I start with the Vanilla, then Chocolate
Wow, Wow, Wow.
There's only one thing left
I eat the Strawberry ice cream
I lick up the rest
It's gone, gone, gone.

Spring 1994

# LA VIE D'UNE FLEUR

Une fleur est pleine de vie
Une fleur a beaucoup de l'amour
Une fleur a besoin d'eau
Les fleurs vivent , il on une cycle de vie
On plante une graine, elle fleurit
Quand son heure s'est passe
Elle droit mourir
Meme si une fleur meurt
Son souvenir demeurre
Jus qu'a ce que quel qu'un l'enleve.

February 1994

# CONSEQUENCES

For every action
There is a reaction
That is a constant
So is learning a constant.
By cheating on something
You only cheat yourself
Not others but only you
I have learned the hard way.
Some advice for students and youth
Always be honest in everything you do
You will succeed even if it takes a little more time
You will go far.
If you cheat yourself it will be with you
For a very long time
You will never forget it.

December 1995

# GOODNIGHT, DEAR ONE

We were frolicking through
The flowers; we were beloved
You made my life richer
With your caring ways
You saved my life over and over
I owe you a heavenly lot
We parted and stayed silent
Not even saying goodbye.
Now I find you again and wonder
Can we turn on our emotions?
Like an old fashioned light switch?
Our time together is and always will be priceless to me.

Spring 1995

# MEMORIES WITH HER

Days were spent in the Jalara jungle
Lovers curling up together like spoons
Never were they entwined
Like the two twin moons
Turning around each other
While glistening from the heat
Only saying what needed to be said.

Spring 1995

# THE WORLD 2

In the world there are animals
They come in all sizes
There's one common thing
They are all earthlings.
Some have different ways of traveling
Others have different markings
They all have their own unique voice
They have many colors.
In the world there are plants
There are those with flowers
That feels wet with the morning dew
Others stay dry to the touch
There are so many species
Plants, birds and reptiles alike
That may go unnoticed or
Undiscovered.
Let us discover the things
That have not been explored
We belong to the planet
That we know so little about
All life forms are unique
They all have faults too
Try to live in harmony
Get along with our comrades on this earth
Keep our planet clean
Our progeny will have a place
To call home that is livable; where the air is fresh
A clean and beautiful land to call home.

Spring 1996

# You're Invisible To Me

You're invisible to me
I cannot say why
You are up north
And yet you are right near me
We walked along
The same muddy path
Somewhere you slipped
I paused and looked back
Saw nothing and continued
You're invisible to me

Spring 1996

# Inside Looking Out

An inclined roof extends from
My window like the peak of a water slide
Opening the window, birds chirp outside
Dew dropped leaves and smells of chimney smoke
Grabbing a handful of raindrops
Cool, slippery and translucent raindrops
Realizing time is passing me by
The present is zooming by like cars on our street
The past won't come again
The future is starting now.

Fall 1996

## Disabling Attacker
Why must it always be me ?
Whom you latch onto and
put down!
If a fly flew by, would you tear
off its wing, disabling it?
If a herd of zebra ran through
your territory,
Would you paint the stripes a
different color, red perhaps?
Why must it always be the
lesser and smaller people you
attack?
The weak against the strong -
Two animals of the same
species confront at a lake
One of them knows how to
swim - the other does not!
Why does it have to be me?

March 1997

Illustrated by: Jason Baker 2010

# COMMUTER TRAIN

Pushing and shoving
Students everywhere in uniforms
Packed train, very little air
People eating oranges and chips
Next stop- who knows?
Little towns, Sweetness
Guys sharing a cigarette outside. Trains.

Fall 1997

# DIFFERENCES

Though the differences are greater
Than we both expected
We ignored all others
Fighting for love against ideals
We thought distance would be all
That which would cure set ideals
For we now know
That distance doesn't matter much
For we are connected at our core
The direct center of our being
Connected, our bodies with each other's
Emotions are not linear
Nor are they logical
Distance is not related
Emotions will shine through
We are apart but still we are connected like rubber cement
Cemented at our hearts and our minds linked.

November 1997

# LES REFLECTIONS

Les rides, les rides qui flottent loin
Qui rament des souvenirs et des cauchemars
Les rides, les rides.
En regardant dans l'eau on voit en courant le contenant
Ils nous passent en force dans l'autre direction
En Navigant tres loin; les rides partout
Quel qu'un lance un caillou
Il va tombe dans l'eau, au milieu
De la piscine, les rides
Qui fait les rides qui s'explosent
Quelque fois fort ou doucement
Ces rides sont les humains
Le caillou et une bombe
L'eau est la paix
Ca c'est ce qu'on doit atteindre
Au lieu des bombes et la guerre.

Fall 1997

# MY HEALER

Now I am healed running into the water
Finding Aphrodite waiting - waiting just for me.
My journey, skipping - through the fields
Fields of strawberries
Berries for my enjoyment.
Jumping through the silver zero
Into a land full of joy and love
Following my internal directions
Through the whole in the zero.
Hopping through the wrought iron gates
To the city in gold beyond
Filled with gold and bronze
Healing me with light.
Coming back to reality slowly
Delaying, swimming with Aphrodite
Smiling with complete
Complete familiar surroundings.
Now I am healed
With the help from a dolphin
Healing me, loving me.

Fall 1997

# LINKED DESTINY

It was meant to be this way for a reason
They say that love is blind and lovers blinded
Were we blind to love? Or to the world?
Were we just not looking close enough?
True love is capable of lasting seconds or
Even multiple lifetimes
For time is irrelevant- man made
We can make it through time and distance
Making it fly by, fly higher than the eagles
Run like a greyhound
Swim and jump like dolphins in the sea
If it was meant to be we will know
By each other's heart
For we are connected at the center
Connected at our heart
My love is never-ending.

October 1997

# LONELIEST PLACE

Sitting here on what seems to me
To be the loneliest place there is
I am here however- watching people go by
Here I go and here I stay
Sitting on a rock and a hard place
This place is here forever
However, I will not be here as long
As this solid stone is smooth from seawater
Flowing over it day by day
By night this is here always
Sitting here waiting for something to happen
Shall I stay until it does?

November 1997

# PAPER CLIP LOVE

You filled my world with love
Emptied the unkindness and despair
Out of my being-
Filling me with joy and happiness
The joy brought back from
The long sojourn someplace else
Love and peace now return to my soul
For which I am eternally grateful
Intermittently sending you a percentage
Of the greatest love, peace and joy
That I had forgotten that I had
And had shoved aside
While flowers and trees die
My for you will never end
For we are attached at the center
Like paper clips in a linked row.

November 1997

# LE MOT DE MON ENFANT

J'ai voyage lointain
Je cherchais des reponses des questions de la vie
J'etais stupifie par combien de ces reponses j'ai trouves
J'ai regarde en Californie et Colombie Britannique
Au Quebec et au New York aussi
En effet les autres humains avaient les memes questions
Qu'ils voulaient poser aux autres
Quand je suis arrivee chez moi
J'ai trouve que ma vie coulait
Et que je n'ai pas trouver une reponse a mes questions
Quand j'etais sur mon lit de mort
Mon enfant ma dit la seule reponse qui m'inquettait
La question c'etait :
Est-ce que j'air fait une difference, Est- ce que j'ai aide?
La reponse etait un mot tres simple maid profonde
C'etait la derniere chose que j'ai entendu - OUI !

Spring 1997

# LES FLOCONS DE NEIGE

Les temps qu'on a passé ensemble
Est comme des flocons de neige
En tombant d'une arbre
Chaque une est differente
Flocons se passent en avant de nos yeux
Les yeux bleues, et bleues-gris
Les yeux ouverts en regardent
Les flocons et les feuilles qui tombent
D' arbustres qu'on a poussé d'une graine
On les voies toutes
C'est exceptionnelle la façon que
Deux personnes qui sont si differentes
Mais en-dessous on est si semblable
Peuvent reacter comme s'est passé
Les coeurs ont été libèré de leurs cages
Les coeurs s'ouvrent sans jugement, sans opinions
Pour moi ça signifie un destin qui á nous presenter.

December 1997

# NUITS SANS COEUR

Les nuits qui s'en viennent serront
Les plus difficiles mais
On va les gagner - notre amitie
Avec aucun vagues a sursauter
Les jours que je m'ennuie
Au milieu de ça, je pense á vous
Des pensées que je ne veut pas oublir
Les nuits sans coeur
C'est les nuits que vous n'êtes pas là
A côté de moi en me parlant
Des choses qui se passent
Les nuits sans vous sont
Des nuits sans coeur.

December 1997

# IT WAS MEANT TO BE

It was meant to be
I feel it in my soul, in my bones
True love is capable of
Lasting decades or only seconds
For time is IRRELEVANT, man made
We can make it through time and distance
We will surely see
If it was meant to be
The quality and amount of our contact
Will tell if this is true
Even though we are linked together
Linked at the center
Words can clutter or they can clarify
Expressing words and feelings
Over great distances
Still we are linked with our hearts.

December 1997

# UNIVERSE AND ME

I have changed much since the moving of the planets
New axis and new air moving people around
Rules and processes changing every day
Practising how to be me every day.
Hiding forever dodging social events
Used to be me in years gone by.
Those social events, the making of friends
Introducing myself to others
Had to be learned by me as fear came trembling down
My spine and my breath quickened pulse increased
Speeches would need to be done, I could do them
Still the fear held me captive most of the time
Held hostage by inhibitions and past experiences
Set free by the occasional encouragement
My will was not strong then
To succeed, to speak out, to cheer others on when I might.
Living with people who have patience, knowing that
They took the time to listen and hear what I really was about
Helping me at every turn, steering me in the right direction.

Fall 1998

# DISTANCE

I wish with all my heart
Upon a shining star
You were here
Here with me
Hearing your voice
So sweet and caring
Yet so far away
Far from my reach
I yearn to hold your hands
To have you near
Just to be with you
The distance between us
I hold you dear in my heart
Now and forever, I promise
I'll be with you someday
I'll be by your side someday
Someday soon.

October 1998

# FROM ME TO YOU

A word when you're lonely
A guide when you're searching
Someone who shares your laughter
Someone who shares your tears
Someone who understands you
Someone whom you need in difficulties
Someone who knows your tears
Someone you love to be with
Someone who makes you smile
Will never be out of style
That's what a special friend is
And here's how you know it's true
Because I am a friend of yours.

October 1998

# CONFLICTS

Conflicts resolve people into acting
Changing something, somehow
People cannot resolve something in themselves
Only time, caring and support can cure these

February 1999

# HIGH AND LOW

At a time in my life
Feeling low and grayish
Searching for my river
My path to follow- to dream
Of successes to come
My path has been mucky
Soiled with puddles
Ankle deep in water
Trying to escape
Reading books helped me through
At one point in my life
Lows and highs succeeded each other
Quickly like a hummingbird in flight
Above a succulent flower.

April 1999

# THE REAL ME

You see me walking down the street
Stop and say hello if my head hangs low
If I appear to be happy - look again
For deep inside may be anger or fear
Inside you may see something
You may see the real me.
You stop and ask me why
I am humming a war song
I reply that I do not know
In my most deep thoughts
You will find all answers
The Real Me.
In my life I wear many masks
Some of which aren't clear
Others are definitely transparent
They show the world the Real Me.
Get to know me, calm me down
Make me feel at ease, I will respond
Take off the masks one by one
I may let you see the Real Me.

April 1999

# LONELY IN THOUGHT

Lonely as I have ever been
Feeling this way as I am here
Empty because I am without
My littlest angel
School is going all right
Success will come my way
Time is all I need and discipline
By myself and me, my lord and my friend
The angels above me - hovering at the ready to assist
I am calling to those who care
To help me, please!
For I know that I need-
Someone to watch over me.

May 1999

# CE QUE JE VOIS

Les rues autours de moi
Le vent au toit
Arbustre sur droite
Une chaîne sur la gauche
Pour moi je les voies
Les toits vert, rouge et gris
Les lumières au coin
Je vois les oiseaux
L'eau viens de la piscine
S'en va par les trous de la piscine
En les regardent je vois
Ce qu'ils veulent
La porte s'ouvre et ils s'en vont
Je regarde les arbres
Le vent autour de moi
Les rues s'enferment
Comme une boite autour de moi.

October 1999

# MY FAMILY AND HOME

Reuniting, becoming clearer, calmer
Family coming together again
Coming into my heart from far away
Friends are family too at my core
My home is being filled with family
With joyous love and wisdom
Members and friends that had been forgotten
My home and my family together again as a whole.
Generations gone by taught their young
To fly away early and find a mate
Who would bring prosperity and wealth
As well as offspring to the family to keep their lineage going
People missed the point, most marriages were moot
Youth in my generation believe that it is a choice
To love, care for and marry a person regardless of gender or sex
To work or serve a spouse, to help others and to love one another
There is growth in this realization and wisdom too.

March 2000

# PEACE & WAR

Peacefully sitting in class
Listening to tanks
Filled with people who want to help
Our country under attack
The younger children were fearful
The others cheered them up
Telling them that it will be okay
While bombshells are flying
Just overhead.

September 2001

# EXPLORER

Out of the darkness - I heard a shout
You came from around the tree
And smiled at me
Bright and wise; smart and deep
The light through which my candle shines
Though our time on this spinning globe is short
Our paths crossed and so began our journey
Whether be short or lasting
Am sure that we will see
The beauty that was meant to be.

Fall 2001

# Alone on a Special Day

There came a time when
I could have left you
Without telling you
Just how much I care
There are no words to express it
I would have died for you
Instead, you died for me
I guess that shows just how much
You cared for me
You stood in line like you should have
Then you took a stand, and lost your life
It's my first year without you
On this Special Day
I wish I could say, "happy valentine's day!"

Spring 2002

# WHAT CHILDREN ARE

Children are our legacy
They show us right from wrong
Through the things they do
They have an ability to cheer us up-
When no one else can-
They are our kids.
They allow us to be vulnerable sometimes
Kids do not judge us by our appearances
Kids show us how to be heroes
Children have courage and wisdom
That sometimes is uncanny.
You see things in them that you
May not like in yourself
Others that you can't explain-
Kids are like mirrors and textbooks
You learn every step of the way.
Legacies left - History passed on and on
Family created and molded;
To be loved and to love in return
This is what children are;
Children are love and lifelong learning.

May 2003

# CHERISHED FRIENDSHIPS

Yesterday, my friend listened to what I had to say
Reassured me, telling me that it'll be okay
My beliefs were shaky, yet I accepted her reply
Hearing those words uttered with affection
Made all my worries fade away.
When my world was falling apart
Words of courage were spoken
Enough to make my fears go away
Supporting me in the trials of life and love
Yesterday, my friend was there.
Reconnecting with ones you love
Speaking as though time had stood still
Reaching out, smiling, knowing
Letting me know again it'll be okay
Today, my friend is back again.
Worlds apart with hearts aglow - connected
Friendships never seemed so harmonious
Waiting for an old message in a bottle
That was tossed in the ocean
Dear One, Will you be there tomorrow?

September 2008

# JOURNEY THROUGH TIME

Throughout my years on this Earthly plane
I have known deep down that I had
A soul mate out there somewhere
Question was would I find her?
After years of searching
Exploring some of the places on this Earth
My spirit had been shattered to its core
By prior experiences and attackers
Whom I thought I loved- had hurt me
How much longer do I have to wait?
Nearing the point of giving up
That is when I found her!
Where? Right where she had been all along
Right under my nose! So to speak, of course...
However, the timing was not quite right
How long would I have to wait?
With eyes vibrant with life's sparkle
A door opened just beyond to her soul
The connection intensified -
Waiting for her to be mine once again.

January 2009

# FEELINGS FROM FOREVER

I was feeling all this love
So I wrote her a poem
Professing my love for this lady
Promising her my undying love
Nothing could become if it until later
Knowing that the feeling had come out from forever
Finding me and her together
Only for a second did I hear
Her love for me, that was there
It was there.
Seeing her bow shaped smile
Azure colored eyes smiling at me daily
Aglow with life and love
I caught many of her glances
I always replied.
My love for her has remained untattered
It has evolved but remained pure
Everlasting, sensual and true in nature
Her lilting sweet voice rings in my ears
Thinking about her holding me close
Rocking back and forth - cuddling up
My heart beats faster, my blue eyes aglow with hope
Still recalling her footsteps, the sound of her walking
Down the halls and into the room each day
Longing for her touch and to hear her voice once again
Makes my heart and soul tingle
Knowing that her love for me has remained
My love, will you speak with me again?

February 2009

# IMZADI, MY SOUL MATE

My heart is pounding- too fast, too strong
Don't know how to slow it down
Wondering if it's happening to her too
At one time her eyes lit up when she saw
That I was in the room
Speaking softly to me, with a gleaming smile
Though boundaries were not crossed
The day we parted ways was hard for me
I needed to grow, to self-realize
Parting was such sweet sorrow- amputating
Not knowing when our hearts would
Once again be one
There have been loveless and abusive situations
Learning somehow, growing
I kept the love I have for her alive.
Here I am – Arms wide open
Waiting and wanting you near me once again
Different context, higher emotions
Yearning to hold you close in my arms
Shower you with love and affection
Like you had shown me years before
Different context, different movie, same hearts
Freely connecting to each other
Our friendship and affection has been sustained
Through written word, with hopes of reconnecting
For an opportunity to create more memories
Always.

Spring 2009

# THE ROSE THORN

Rose thorn - shapely, unique.
the prickling sensation of blood flowing
Like a volcano erupting.
The colloidal liquid is like red wine mixed with milk
Trying to clean itself and re-cover itself with new human skin.
The covering process is like a jigsaw puzzle,
Healing piece by piece and layer by layer.
It's wonderful and frightening-
This could happen again.

Spring 2009

# Recipe of Life for a Girl

If you are a girl there are thing
That are expected of you
Throughout your lifetime by others
Wearing cute dresses, going to Sunday services
Having long hair and braids or pig tails
Doing well at creative arts and poorly at math
These are things that are expected by others.
If you are a girl and not performing or doing
Any of these things, not wearing dresses for example
Then you may get teased and taunted by others
Perhaps throughout your life because they don't understand
That everyone is
an individual and not every girl likes dresses
That girly girl stuff gets to be too much for some girls.
Then in those cases, a parent and friends must make exception
Know and love the girl for who she is and not what she wears
Or for how she does her hair
Then a true friendship may evolve.

Spring 2009

# TRUE FRIENDSHIPS ARE BETTER THAN FAMILY

Special friendships can last a lifetime
A true friend is there for you
Always - for venting, for sharing a ride to work
Talking 'till 2 in the morning about girl stuff
A friend will be there when you need them
To console you, to comfort you best they can.
A true friend doesn't expect birthday cards every year
For they know they are being sent warm wishes from afar
Or they call each other on that special day
And they know that they are always loved by the other.
A true friend is felt like family - only better because
You choose your friends, you rarely choose your family
Friendship is a partnership of hearts
Caring and sharing stories and woes
Joyous events and sorrows
True friendships last, decades or lifetimes
May our hearts join in friendship always.

Spring 2009


End of Section 1

# SECTION 2:

# SHORT STORIES & JOURNALS

# Liquid Sunshine

One night my family and I went for supper with other resort guests, and a dinner show at White River. We were in Jamaica, and the natives were going to put on a cultural show for the people staying at the resort. This show was about two hours on a bus, then a ride on a small boat along a torch lit, curvy river. The whole evening was to be under the stars but there were drops of 'liquid sunshine' as they called it during supper. As the native show went on, the rain got heavier, to a point where we had to run for shelter. By midnight the drops were like golf balls, and we had no choice but to go back to the resort- the way we had come in the small boat. On the dark and curvy river to the bus that would take us back to the resort we were all staying in.

The people driving the boat and the bus had a 'devil may care' attitude; we sang our hearts all the way back. Jamaica's 'liquid sunshine' gave us an evening that we will long remember.

Spring 1986

# MELISSA THE EASTER BUNNY

Once there was an Easter Bunny, named Melissa. One day she flew to the moon to get some golden Easter eggs. She flew back down to Earth and put them into the baskets. She put one of the golden eggs into each of her baskets. For everyone knows that a bunny can only hold so many baskets! Each bunny has an appointed route on Easter Sunday. Melissa had about a dozen homes to go to where there were children waiting. The children were surprised to receive a golden egg in the morning. From then on, there were a few golden eggs handed out each year to the children who would appreciate them, in the memory of that one Easter morning.

Spring 1987

# MY GRANDDAD, MY FAVORITE PERSON GRADE 2 QAIS SPEECH

Do you have a Granddad to love? Well I do! He is my favorite person. My Granddad is my mom's dad. He used to give me a lot of peppermints which he kept In his pocket. He used to sit and read to me. Granddad enjoyed nature, reading and working in his vegetable garden. The sad thing is that Granddad ate too much junk food and cheese was his favorite food. His arteries became clogged. Two years ago he died, but we know he has gone to a better place. I miss him a lot. I will keep his memories alive. Best of all my Granddad was kind and loving.

Winter 1988

# THE LEPRECHAUN'S GOLD

On the night of St. Patrick's day at my house, my family and I were looking at slides. When we got to about the 100th slide, a leprechaun appeared right in front of my view of the slideshow. I went over to ask him to move. He answered like this, "Yes, I will move, but I want to know your name." I told him my name was Laurie, then he introduced himself, "My name is Patrick, I want to have a race with you to see if you can beat me". I asked him to come closer to me, and asked him to explain further. "I want you to race with me to the place I have hidden the gold". I asked him to show me his map and explained the maps legend. There was a house drawn in the upper left corner and had dashes and arrows pointing around the house and into the neighbor's yard where there was a big tree. This tree was a huge oak tree, that marked the lot line. The arrows went around the tree in a circle and then went towards a bridge. This little bridge went over a stream that separated the two streets and led to one of the main roads in the county. Patrick them pointed to a bunch of mountains at the upper right of the map. He told me that the pot of gold was hidden someplace near the mountains. There was a rainbow over the mountains and a black cauldron on the map, which as the legend indicated, was the pot of gold. It seemed to be a long trip for a ten-year-old girl to do by herself.

Around the tree and along the highway, and around or through the mountains. I decided to do it, after checking with the parents of course. They said that they would get the money from the pot of gold, because I was too young to handle money at the time. I arranged with them that it would be put into a safe holding account. However, the leprechaun told me that I would only get a share of the pot of gold, because he did not want to empty his supply as it was bad luck to not have any gold in his pot.

The race was set for the next day, and Patrick said that the average human could do the race in about three hours. If they could find the pot's location and get to the mountain without asking for help along the way from other people or animals. I ended up winning the race, with a few minutes to spare! I jumped out of excitement when I won the race. Suddenly I realized that it had all been a dream. Mom and dad were still looking at slides, one of a scuba diving trip and a sunken ship with gold bars and other trinkets. Whoa! Was I disappointed!

Spring 1988

# CAR TRIP MEMORIES

I used to ride in the back of one of mom's cars and I thought it was fun and really cozy. The car was a medium shade of blue almost everywhere throughout the car. The make and model was a 1982 Nissan Maxima and it had blue plush seats. Lighter than royal blue, but darker than sky blue it calmed me when I was inside. Even the seatbelts were blue, with silver buckles. I really liked her car. It had soft plush material on the seats and it was very comfortable for sleeping in. On long car trips, I would cuddle up in the back seats and gaze up at the trees and the stars as we drove. Most of the time this would lull me into a sleep. I would hear the music playing in the car, and sometimes I even had a blanket to keep me warm. The car had an automated voice that would tell us if the "key is in the ignition" or if the "deck is ajar" which helped me feel more secure. Riding in mom's car gave me a sense of security and calmness which brought stability into my life. So for a short time, no one could take her car from me.

Spring 1988

# THE SMALLEST CHRISTMAS TREE

The Dennison children were decorating their Christmas tree. The little mouse was watching them from his mouse hole in the family room wall. Father mouse wanted a tree too, so did the little ones. They were sad that they could not get one because the trees were so big. That night while father mouse was scrounging for crumbs and food bits left out by the Dennison's he saw something he'd never seen before. There, right in front of him, was a bushy, green branch of the Christmas tree. It was just big enough for him to pick up with his teeth. Father mouse decided that it would be perfect for his family's Christmas tree, after all a mouse can't buy things from a store to put under the tree. When he dragged it into the mouse's hole, mother mouse saw the tree branch and rushed away and came back with a few pieces of popcorn that had fallen off the big tree. Together they worked to put the popcorn onto the branch. On Christmas morning, the baby mouse could not believe his eyes! There in front of him was a beautiful Christmas tree branch that his parents had decorated. They had placed some bits of cheese and crumbs underneath that served as their gifts and their breakfast. That was the happiest and most bountiful Christmas the mice ever had!

Fall 1989

# *QUAND?* A SCHOOL PUBLIC SPEAKING COMPETITION SPEECH

Quand. Un mot. Quand j'etais jeune. Quand j'avais peur. Quand je jouais. Mme. Superieur, juges honorables, parents, professeurs et amis etudiants, je vais vous parlez d'un mot avec cinq lettres, qui est le mot "quand". Je peux dire beaucoup avec ce mot. On sert du mot "quand" comme une adverbe pour introduire un temps en particular - par example,

"Quand est-ce que j'ai laisse mon enfance?", ou "Quand est-ce que j'ai arrete de jouer avec mes poupees?" Dans ses examples on peut remplacer le mot "quand" par "a quel moment". Le mot "quand" peut etre uniliser aussi comme une conjunction - par example, "Quand j'etais jeune je rirais beaucoup parce que la vie etait belle", ou "Quand j'avais peur, je fermais mes yeux." On peut remplacer le mot quand par "lorsque".

On emplois le mot "quand" pour parler du passe, de present, ou du future. Maintenant que j'ai dis tout que je voulais dire, j'ai une question, quand est-ce que je vais finir mon discours?

Spring 1990

# *SWEET SUGAR* A QAIS SPEECH

While on holiday in Florida recently, I saw something I won't soon forget. I had the pleasure of meeting a pet dolphin called Sugar. The hotel had closed off an inlet from the ocean to form a pond and that is where Sugar lived. When we arrived, we were told that Sugar's trainer was away on vacation. He had trained her to do tricks to get her food, so three times a day, Sugar put on a show for the hotel guests. While Robert was away, his daughter Debby, did the tricks with Sugar. Sugar's trained behaviour remained perfect, but the change in her personality had everyone worried. Normally in her free time, Sugar would swim to the sides of the pond to greet anyone who came near, by lifting her head out of the water and saying hello in dolphin talk. Now, Sugar just swam around the center of the pond; unhappy, pouting and paying no attention to anyone, probably because she missed Robert so much.

When Robert returned home, he sat by the pond petting Sugar and walking to her. Before long, she began jumping out of the water diving, waving her fins and saying hello to everyone. Sugar was indeed back to normal, her personality became sweet again because the one she loved has returned.

Spring 1990

# THE DREAM OF MOUNT WALKER

One day there was a girl named Michelle who loved to walk up and down small mountains and hills. She had climbed almost everyone in her area. Mount Walker was the one she had not dared to walk as it was more than twelve thousand feet above sea level. She always dreamed she would do it one day. Michelle was now in her mid-twenties and was determined to do the climb to Mount Walker. Michelle was in college one day and started to daydream. Michelle was an outdoor recreation major in college, and loved climbing both in reality and in her dreams. This particular day was quite boring as the professor was going over rules for tree climbing and rock climbing. "Michelle, where is the north on the compass, and how do you find it?" the professor asked Michelle as she was deep into her daydream. Michelle realized that she was being asked a question and she opened her eyes and began to answer the question by drawing in the air with her finger, the wind direction gauge. Then she described where the North was in relation to the room they were in.

The professor did not like that she had to use the wind direction gauge to figure it out, after all Michelle was in her final year of classes now and should know that off by heart. Michelle apologized and explained that she was a visual learner and used the gauges whenever she could to help her figure things out. That seemed to get the professor off her back for a while. So, Michelle went back into her revelry and finished her climb to the peak of Mount Walker.

Fall 1990

# A STEP ALONG MY SOUL'S JOURNEY

e were driving on the way home from school one day on the school bus when something unusual happened. We were driving along a quiet suburban neighborhood in the Montreal area, I was sitting on my seat as usual talking to one of the students next to me. Vanessa and Leigh and Lindsay were within sight of where I was sitting on the bus. The Quebec roads were terrible, pot hole city, you might call it. Each time we went over a pot hole larger than a Frisbee, we all would bounce up out of our seats a little bit. At the next stop, the bus driver opened the door and a lady wearing a powder blue sweater and a taupe-green skirt asked if I was on the bus and the driver replied that I was and pointed back to where I was sitting. We kept on driving to school. The lady came back and started talking to me. "Is your mother in school these days?", I thought about this and answered the lady. "No, in fact she finished her schooling," I paused and then added "you'll probably be able to reach her at home if you are looking to talk to my mom". At the next stop the lady got out of the bus, and I talked to the bus driver for a few minutes as I often would. After a few moments went by, I noticed my throat was getting a little bit dry and felt like it was pringly, like pins and needles in one's feet.

I reached into my mouth to see what it was. I felt some kind of vine in my mouth, rooted at my palate and dangling down into my chest through my throat. It felt like rose vine or something that was just as rough, but not as pointy - I could not identify it right away. I wondered why it was there in the first place. I sort of knew that my unconscious dreams could be sending me messages or allowing me to express something or learn something from the world. I pulled at the vine for what seemed like a few moments, after a few strong yanks and feeling like it would never de-root from my palate, I finally got it out of my mouth. But the question remained, what was it and how did I get that vine growing in my mouth in the first place? It was coming up to my stop and as usual I had d to tell the driver I wanted to get off, the words would not come out. I was blocking again - oh no! I was probably going to miss my stop. I was getting off at another stop, not my usual one at the corner of our street. This one was just past the Harpell center and the highway overpass. While trying to get the words out of my mouth, I saw my teacher from the previous year, Mary Palo walking underneath the overpass. I opened the window nearest me and waved at her saying hello. Having gotten the hello out of my mouth in time, I decided to not waste the energy and ask the driver to let me off the bus at the next corner. Getting off the bus finally, I ran to where Mary Palo had headed. I caught her in the train station parking lot and we chatted for a few moments, before I told her I had to get where I was supposed to be. She encouraged me to speak, telling me that I had valued opinions and that it was time for me to speak out. So after hearing those words of encouragement, I identified the vine that had been in my mouth. It was thyme - as in the universe telling me it was time to speak, that uprooting the vine and taking the vine out of my mouth would allow me to speak again without blocking or any other impediment.

Summer 1990

# FINGERLINGS VISIT KUPER ACADEMY

O ne morning halfway through spelling class some grade five students heard an unusual noise coming from outside. A young blonde haired girl named Melanie went to the window and saw a Frisbee shaped space ship that was landing in the school playground. An elevator type door opened and many eight-inch-high greenish blue aliens came rushing out of the ship on two legs. They stood still and appeared to be conversing. They were hovering about a foot off the ground, moving towards the school's front door. When they got closer to the school the students could see that they had elf like features- the ears and eyes, but they also had a non elf feature. Their nose and mouth were similar to that of a baboon and some students commented that they could see a tail trailing behind these creatures.

The aliens went right to the students in grade five and six, because they wanted to find an earthling who knew how to communicate effectively in English. Most of all they wanted someone who could use this thing they had found on their planet years before. Which was a long-wooden shaped thing with a point at the end, yellow in color and beige at the tip. Apparently it had been left on their home world many years prior to their current visit. Their scientists and government officials wanted to display this item in their Museum of Other Worlds, but wasn't sure what it was or how to use it. All they knew was it was made out of wood and that it could be rolled around on flat surfaces. However, they could not pick it up or use it as they didn't know what it was supposed to be. They had named the pencil something else in their language. Miss McNamara's class was intrigued and awestruck that these aliens could speak and understand English, because they were off-world residents. The creatures explained that air waves had finally reached their planet about 12 years ago and they had studied most of our language. The class was finally being let-in on the big government cover ups about aliens on Earth.

They noticed that Miss McNamara was dressed differently than the others in the class and seemed to be older, so the aliens assumed that she may be in charge there, and asked her if they could spend some time observing the class to learn about us and to learn how to use the pencil. The teacher and students all agreed and said they would teach these aliens to write with pencils that afternoon. They spent the afternoon with us, sitting or floating nearby- wherever they could see what we were doing. They explained that the reason they had chosen an educational institution was that they had seen that our school was called Kuper Academy and explained that the element copper was one of their most prized things on their home world.

The aliens identified themselves as Fingerlings, at least that was the English name for their species. At the end of the day, the Fingerlings were sad to go but they needed to get back before they forgot what they had learned for their short term memory was not very good. They asked if they could bring someone to their planet for a weekend to teach at their education center which was inside of the museum. They promised they would have the person back the following weekend. Melanie volunteered to go, but had to call her mother first to get the okay. After getting the okay from her mother, they left the school after saying goodbye. Melanie went with them to their planet. The journey seemed to take about five hours. After settling in to her assigned sleeping quarters in the museum, Melanie got to teaching the residents how to pick up, and use a pencil. She decided to name their education center after her elementary school. Melanie called the new education center, "Kuper's Alien Academy".

The Fingerlings upheld their promise and had Melanie back at her home the following weekend. On Monday morning Melanie regaled her teacher and class all about her off-world adventure. They were all jealous, of course.

Written 1992, Revised 2009

# MY GREAT UNCLE

My mother told me that my grandmother knew someone who is heroic. While great uncle Bill was driving along a road in Ontario, he saw fire engines and ambulances going by. He decided to follow them to see what was going on. He followed the trucks around for about ten minutes. They stopped in front of a house that was engulfed in flames. Since Bill had studied one year to be a firefighter, he asked the responders if they would need a hand. He mentioned he had studied for a year and knew how to do a rescue. When the flames were almost out, one firefighter went up the front of the building to try to bring out two people that were trapped inside. When he brought one of the people down, the person said there was one more person inside on the second floor. Bill suggested that he should attempt to bring the second person out of the house, as it is not good to subject oneself to smoke inhalation twice in one short period. The firefighter told him he would give him his gear and reminded him of the risks. Bill climbed the ladder and saw the person standing in the back room on the second floor, they were young and obviously having trouble breathing. Bill went down slowly as he had to hold on to the person. On the way down the person passed out, possibly from inhaling too much smoke. When they reached the ground, Bill started rescue breathing. After five minutes, the person started to react and breathe on their own. As was the procedure, they took the person to the hospital for observation and to get checked for other damage. The next week my grandmother saw his picture in the newspaper on the front page.

Spring 1992

# A DAY TRIP WITH MY FAMILY

There is one event that I will never forget in my entire life. It happened one day when I was six years old when my family took a day trip. My parents and my uncle John and I went on a day trip to Park Safari in Hemmingford, Quebec in the summer of 1986. We had planned this trip for about a week and it was otherwise a great day, good weather and sunshine shining in the sky. When we got to the park it was sunny and there were almost no clouds, we made sure to go on all the rides and fed most of the animals we could. Park Safari was known as one of the sights to see in the region, and I had been going with my parents biannually. However, this trip would turn into one that was unforgettable. There was only one ride left to go on and that was the ferris wheel, we lined up and waited for about an hour. We were finally allowed to get on the ferris wheel and when we got to the top of the wheel clouds moved in and it started to drizzle! We became impatient and worried about the weather. We were still on the ferris wheel when it started to rain very hard.

The man who operated the wheel started to let people out, unfortunately for us we were at the top! We were getting soaked from our heads down to our sandals. The wheel then stalled about half way down to the ground, and then my family and I started to worry as we got drenched by rain. The operator man ran to get help and within a few moments the ride was working again. When we were off and back on the ground, dad made sure we were all right and though we all were cold and wet, we were not injured. We made a b-line to the car, after uncle John wrapped his sweater around me to make sure I would be warm. Once at the car the first thing he did was turned on the heating system so we would not catch colds on the way back home to Montreal. Despite the negative ending to our day, we drove home feeling like we had an adventure that we would never soon forget however feeling disappointed that we didn't get to complete our ride as we would have hoped - with sunshine and birds singing and my family all around me. We enjoyed our day at Park Safari and still nearly six years later, I remember it well.

October 1992

# MY DECISIONS AT HOME

There was a heated argument between my parents one night at home, a verbal one where voices were raised, and questions asked, while I overheard from my room upstairs through the heating vent in the floor. I ended up being torn and confused about what to do regarding the situation, assuming they would give me a choice, for I knew it was going to turn out the way it did. Making the decision before being asked is always a good way to save yourself from stress and from disappointing too many people at one time. I knew my parents were going to be divorced, and not live together anymore but what I did not know for sure is who I wanted to live with. I had heard stories and watched movies about latch key kids from divorced parents, and hoped that my future would not be like theirs. I went upstairs after supper the next night and made a list of things I liked about both my parents, to help me make my decision easier. In my case, I was closer emotionally with my mom and wanted approval and support from my father.

Weighing the issues, I had with both of them, and imaging the life I would or could have if I decided the other way took a few days for sure. If I went to live with my father in the United States, I would have to leave my school and friends and community perhaps only returning for holidays and summers. This didn't sit well with me but I considered it for the long term benefits. Heeding the thoughts of my father being six hours away by car was also not too pleasant but it was his decision to go there I guess.

Fall 1993

# IN MEMORY OF

Elizabeth Park in West Hartford, Connecticut was filled with people. There was some sitting on the benches or rollerblading, and some were exercising. As people walked in through the park, they walked through a meadow, with an overlook point at the top of a hill. Through the meadow to one side, there was the Rose Garden. There were eight rows of arbors in a circle with beautiful colored roses growing from the ground, up on the trellises. Each type of rose had different fragrances as Melanie had noticed. Melanie was on her way home from school and on her way had stopped at the local healthy restaurant, Mr. Fresser's. Following her light lunch, Melanie headed through the rose garden, smelling honey and jam scented roses along the way. She spotted the gazebo that was where the trellises converged in the center. It had flower pots with alyssums and chrysanthemums on the hexagonal shaped gazebo, which was stained a dark brown color. Melanie saw an unfamiliar face, and decided to go and say hello. A young guy was rollerblading and was trying to go down the stairs on his skates. Melanie said hello and asked if he would like some help. Melanie offered her hand for him to balance while attempting to skate down the stairs. "Thanks. My name is Steven. I live around the corner," the guy replied. "I'm Melanie. I live pretty close too." Melanie smiled at Steven Melanie asked what he was doing in the park and he replied that he was a volunteer and liked to come and skate on his days off. He tended the rose garden and the camp sites nearby. Melanie was very interested in plant life and animals so she asked him if he would take a walk with her around the duck pond. The pond was peanut shape in which weeds grew and reeds grew sometimes overgrowing and spreading onto the grasses. People who walked by admired the ducks and sometimes had picnics on the tables nearby.

Steven told Melanie on their walk that he played trumpet and French Horn with the school band. Melanie told him that she too was in the band and played saxophone and clarinet. Steven told Melanie that he had lived about 15 minutes away from her home in Montreal. By the time that they walked back around to the gazebo, it was almost time for supper. He told Melanie to be at the park tomorrow, at the same time with her saxophone. They would play in the rose garden. Then, he leaned over and gave her a sweet innocent kiss on her cheek. When they played in the park the next day, they had a big audience, at least it seemed like it was a big audience. After they had played one set Melanie said that she was going back home to Montreal for two weeks. She said that she would come back soon to play music with Steven again. Next time she would bring her clarinet- as it was easier to transport. Three months later when she came back from her mom's home, Melanie went to the park to find Steven. He was nowhere to be seen. She went inside the volunteer office, into the room where the people left their personal belongings in lockers while they worked. There was a locker that had black marks on it, and rust at the bottom. She saw a golden plaque saying 'In Memory Of..' and bent down to read it. It was too shocking to finish. 'Steven LeClaire- volunteer of two years' is what it read and then.... '1970-1994'. He had died just a few weeks before.

September 1995

# LET'S PUT OUR MINDS TOGETHER

O ne night the greatest fear of a family became reality when their nineteen-year-old son, William was beaten up so badly that he had to be rushed to the General Hospital. He had to undergo many hours of surgery to try to patch things together his broken body. Amazingly he survived the surgery, but went into a deep coma afterwards.

William was a nice young man but had hanging out with the wrong crowd. William was in room 511 with two other people. Margaret, a middle aged married woman who had gone through heart surgery and James, an older man who had received a kidney transplant and was not responding very well. The nurses went about their duties, checking up on their patients every hour. The situation in room 511 looked very grim. William had been in a coma for just over a week. He was reliving his entire life in his dreams but on the outside he looked like a lifeless vegetable. William's mother, Nancy, had started a natural health school in 1991. The school was based on natural healing abilities and on spirituality. The first class of healers had graduated the previous year and student enrollment had increased to about two hundred from about fifty.

Nancy had talked to one of her students and friends about her son's condition. He then decided he would get a distant healing chain and a prayer line going for her and her son's recovery. He contacted most of the graduates from the previous year and some of the current students who had completed the energy work courses. He told them of the situation and that Nancy was really upset and distraught. He was that they contact their friends too if they knew of any that would add Nancy's son to their prayers. Graduates were asked to send Nancy and her son some healing white light, which is the purest, rescue light to send intentionally to someone for healing. The prayers were directed to both Nancy and Williams angels and spirit guides, many people agreed to spend one hour starting at seven o'clock on Saturday night concentrating on William's recovery. At about a quarter to nine on Saturday night, the nurses went on their rounds to check on their patients in room 511. As she entered she felt something was different, almost as though the room was filled with people. She started to hear beeping sounds, so she checked the instrumentation. William then opened his eyes and looked up at her and smiled. He appeared to be awakening from a beautiful dream. Incredibly Margaret, half sitting at the time, asked the nurse to help her to her feet; then James wanted to know if he could have something to eat. The nurse rushed back to the nurse's station to report these remarkable recoveries and improving conditions only to hear that the other nurses discussing the unusual improvements in many of their patients. Just then Nancy and her husband walked in. Nancy said that they had a phone call and were told to come and see William at eight o'clock.

A few moments later the nurses understood what had happened in room 511, and only half believing in esoteric studies, told them of the effects surrounding the other patients. The energy and healing prayers had indeed worked and in fact had radiated hopeful energy to other patients. Everyone involved had their faith in miracles renewed. William is now at home, doing physiotherapy and getting stronger each day. His life and others' has been transformed because of a Saturday night spent in room 511.

Spring 1995

# MY FIRST TWO FRIENDS

I f you have a close friend in life then you are lucky, especially if this friend is a true friend that stays with you through thick and thin. My first good, close friend was Preeti. She is from an Indian family with whom I have become a third child. We were in pre-school when we met originally after our parents agreed that it would benefit both of us greatly. We were skeptical about how long our friendship would last as pre-school only lasts a couple of years at most. We stayed very close friends until grade four, when I changed schools and left the immediate area where I grew up.

We re-connected in grade seven, when I returned to the local public system for one year. Even though we were apart for two years, not spending much time together, we picked up right where we had left off. It was a wonderful feeling to have someone who was like a big sister (she is 4 months older than me) looking out for you at a big public school - that is exactly what she did. She had transferred in to that school earlier than me, as she skipped a grade - so that too had put a bit of distance between us, but I didn't care and she still included me in some of her group hanging times. During the two years that I was at private school, occasional phone calls to check in with each other or spend an afternoon together kept us in touch at least a bit. When she became interested in guys, it again made a bit of distance between us. You see, I knew that I was not into guys at that time, nor did I think I ever could be. I did have a short relationship with a guy in grade seven, and that is when I was sure that I was not heterosexual. Our friendship grew again for a little while during that one year. I once again became part of the extended family, being invited to parties, and to their Indian temple once. I decided to switch back to private school for the rest of high school, and landed up meeting my second best friend. My second best friend is Tabitha, her family and her are Chinese, from Hong Kong. We met in grade eight, and quickly became friends.

We are both shy when it comes to meeting people we don't know, and that somehow bonded us together. Tabitha explained to me that she had been held back a year because her grades were not good enough. She was going to be tutored this year by one of the school administrators and one of the other teachers as well. Tabitha seemed to be nervous when introducing herself to me, so that was another thing that bonded us - as I had speech dyslexia and it took me several additional seconds to speak when put on the spot. Tabitha and I are still fairly close friends, even though we have not hung out together since we graduated high school.

We do keep in touch by email and online messengers and it feels like we can still catch up and speak like we were never apart. I feel very blessed to have had these two friends in my school years. I am hoping to have more friends like these two down the road.

Winter 1996; Edited and added to 2006

# A Whole New Life

One morning in Burbank, California as William Cochrane got up out of bed he heard his little dog bark. His dog was a Pekinese whose name was Zefram. This particular bark usually signified that William was needed at the door. William thought that it's probably just the gazette and mail but decided to go and check it out anyway. When he looked more closely at the envelopes, he saw an unfamiliar hand writing on one of them. He read it aloud as if he was reading the Zefram.

> Dear William,
>
> I am writing in response to your personal ad in last week's newspaper. My name is Kelly O'Brien. I am the kind of woman who likes honest men. I love dancing and going to parties. I live in Glendale at the moment with my younger sister and her Chihuahua, Sally. I am a full time interior decorator and I try to please my customers by selecting pleasing solutions to their design dilemmas. I would like to meet you at a café and get to know one another. You can reach me at lunch around one pm or after work around half past five. My number at work is 032-6423 and my number at home is 026-8231. Hope to see you soon.
>
> Sincerely, signed, Kelly O'Brien

When William finished reading the letter he called home and told his mother about the unusual letter, since he had not posted the want ad in the paper. His mother said that she had posted the ad for him and that she sounded like a nice woman. Zefram got excited too as his human friend got ready to call Kelly. He reached her at work that afternoon. They talked for a while and found they seemed to get along well and decided to get together the following evening. They both seemed to be anxious to meet, as was Zefram, who insisted on licking William's face before he left! (sort of a bon voyage, good luck on the date).

William suggested they meet at a little café called 'The Peach Pit' that was not far from his place around six o'clock the next day. William knew one of the waiters at the café and asked his friend Kenny to wait on them as this was a special date. They arrived separately but almost at the very same time. Both seemed to be pleasantly surprised at how the other looked. William told Kelly that he was a veterinarian in the area and loved animals since he was little and told her about Zefram.

They ate their dinners and drank some California Chablis. Around nine o'clock they decided it was time to go, as the café was closing. William helped Kelly into her car and they parted ways for the night with the hope of seeing each other again.

During the next few months they saw each other several times a week always having a great time together. They found they had more in common each time they met and even though there was a seven-year age difference, they knew they were in love with each other. After six months they decided to get married. They were so sure of their love The announcement of their engagement went to the pages of the gazette where Williams personal ad had been months earlier, with a thank you to the personals editor. Kelly and William felt that the newspaper ad that had brought them together was a gift from destiny. They planned a simple wedding in the spring with their closest friends and relatives.

About eight months later, Kelly Cochrane, formally Kelly y O'Brien, gave birth to twins. Two of the most adorable twins that you ever did see! Kelly and William were made for one another.

Spring 1996

# CENTRY HIGH SCHOOL STAFF 10 YEAR REUNION

T he Centry High School was having a staff reunion in one week. It had been ten years since the LAVA team had worked together all in their third floor office. They and other staff members were getting ready for the big night. One of the LAVA team members was Valerie Pulaski. She was of medium height with silvery grey hair and wore a happy smile most of the time. It had not been that long since she stopped teaching at Centry. Anothermember of the LAVA team was playing on a community sports team. Alex was tall, and had hair the color of a roasted almond. It has been a few years since he had taught at Centry and was thinking about all the different sports teams that he had coached and all the students he had taught. Alex has taught many things, but specialized in English Language Arts. The third member of the LAVA team was Robert Woods. He has brown blushing eyes and shiny brown hair kept off his forehead and a moustache that was half a shade lighter than his hair. He wore glasses most of the time and walked with an odd gait. Robert had an excellent memory and was patient with students as it took a lot to anger him. He was primarily a social science teacher but coached some teams too. The students seemed to enjoy how he made the dry history courses more learnable through his impressions of historical people and political leaders. Robert had left Centry a many years ago. While sitting at home at night, Robert started to remember some of the students that he had taught, that had a lasting impression on him. One of them was Melanie, she had blond hair and bluish eyes and he was remembering how she used to come to pick him up to make sure he would get to class. As he recalled she got average grades, and had a minor speech impediment that slowed her down a bit when she wanted to speak. She used to laugh at the impressions I did, even if they weren't meant to be funny. A few days later, each member was getting ready for the reunion in their own way. Valerie was going to the hair salon. The reunion would be in the gymnasium on Saturday night. The reunion was going to be open to the families of both teachers and administrators. Very few present day staff had been invited. There was going to be music and nice decorations. The next day, the reunion was starting and people were arriving at Centry. The first to arrive were the Traverteen's. Lauren and Steven had made the trip back for this reunion. Steven was the director of the high school and Lauren was one of the senior gym teachers. Steven has shining white hair that was receding. He had a heartwarming smile and a moustache. Lauren has sandy-brown hair and gorgeous blue eyes. Steven went and turned on the party lights. The back sets of lights on the stage were used for such occasions. While Mrs. Traverteen was looking into the phys ed. office at her old desk, she saw the next person to arrive. She was stunned to see that Mr. Lancer has not changed much over the years. She went over to him and said hello.

"Hello, Don." Don replied, "Hi, Lauren. How's it going with you and Steven?"

Mr. Lancer has short brown hair and a smile that would make you think twice before coming close. This could be a good thing, or a bad thing, depending if you were on his good or bad list. Don was a very good phys ed. teacher as well. He was always athletic as he would ride his bike to work most days in the fall and spring. This is how he has arrived today, on his bike with casual clothes on. So he went into the back to change. As Don got back into the physical education area, he saw that Wally had arrived. They had not seen each other for at least one year. Wally had silvery grey hair and vivid blue eyes. He had been a physical education teacher and also taught high school biology and introduction to technology. Wally also had coached several sports teams over the years. Wally could make any-one feel like they were at home, he could make you laugh too if you needed it. The next person to arrive was Valerie. She had put on a three quarter length dress with different shades of blue. It looked stunning on her. Steven walked over to her. "Hello, Valerie. How are you?" Valerie spoke to him and Lauren, who had come over to say hello as well, for a few moments then went to greet Wally and Don. Don Lancer has asked if any of the LAVA team had spoken to each other since the last of them left. Valerie told them that it had been at least three years since they had spoken to one another. She had heard through the alumni updates and through the grapevine that they all were healthy and in good spirits. Alex was the next to arrive with his family. He said hello to Steven and Lauren then continued to make the rounds. He stopped to chat with Valerie. Alex said, "Hi. Long time since we have all been a team, eh?" In response, she told him that she was alright and that she thought the reunion was a great idea.

She asked him how he and his family were. "Family is all well. Thanks for asking. This reunion was a great idea." Alex said to Valerie. Wally had heard about the reunion from Melanie, who had heard it through the grapevine. Wally had seen her at Centennial a few times since she had left Montreal. Wally went over to the phone and dialed the number he had for Melanie. "Hello?" Melanie said over the phone. "Melanie? This is Wally." he said in a semi-formal manner.

"Hi, Wally. How are you? Isn't the reunion tonight?" she asked her friend from Centry. Remembering how in tune with stuff she was, he replied, "Yes, I am in the gym now and some people have already come. Are you in town?" Wally was not sure where she was, as he had called her cellular phone number. "Yes, I am in town. Thanks for calling. I'd be glad to come. See you soon." Melanie said, smiling from ear to ear. She thought they'd never ask! Melanie put on her best dress and did her hair quickly, headed out the door- forgetting to feed her little dog in the process. Melanie could usually count on Wally to keep her up to date. He was a good friend. In the school gymnasium, the disc jockey was there and had set up on the stage. Mary had arrived and her son Kenneth had accompanied her. Mary had been a top notch math teacher at Centennial. She had silvery grey hair and beautiful eyes. She used to get students to leave class if they did not do homework for a few consecutive days. David has also arrived with his wife Carolyn. David had been the head of the middle school and an English teacher.

He had silvery grey hair that was almost all gone by this time. He had moved away a few years back and had not really participated in many events since. He greeted and spoke to everyone and then just mingled. Melanie arrived soon after David had. She noticed that Don Lancer was either avoiding someone, or just having a sit down in the back office. She said hello to Don and Lauren. Melanie explained that she had heard through the grapevine that there may be a reunion, and Wally had called her a while ago to confirm. Melanie walked into the gym and started making the rounds. "Hello Alex. How are you?" she asked Alex.

"Mello! How did you hear about the reunion? Good to see you." He replied, she explained how she had heard and wished him well. Melanie walked over to Valerie, and said hello. Valerie in turn asked how Melanie was to which Melanie replied, "I'm fine, thanks for asking. Wie geht es Ihnen?" Valerie was impressed! "I see you have been working on your German. I'm fine, thanks." Valerie was surprised that Melanie actually made such an improvement in her spoken German like Melanie had said ten years ago Melanie went over to see Wally. "Hi Wally. Thank you for calling me. It's good to be back."

A few moments later the last of the LAVA team arrived. Melanie remembered the sound of Bob's odd gait. There were other footsteps coming with his, she thought that it must be his family. Bob was pleasantly surprised to see who greeted him at the gymnasium doors. "Mel! It's been a while. How are you?" Bob said smiling as usual. Melanie explained that she had heard about the reunion from Wally and said that she was doing well. She had completed her education degree and was working at a wonderful school. Alex came over to say hello to his friend and Mel. Overhearing the newsy update on Mel, he congratulated her and asked where she was teaching. The reply was, "You will find out soon". She had written to the alumni coordinator and asked that she put an update into the Cougar- the alumni newsletter magazine. Carolyn walked by and asked Mel to help her make a new bowl of punch. Melanie told the men that she would come and chat with them again. They went into the new cafeteria and got the supplies and made up the bowl of punch. Melanie brought it back to the table. The reunion party lasted until couple hours after that. The music had been great, oldies and classic songs were played. Most of the staff had promised to stay in touch and had exchanged contact information. Melanie said that she would be planning a school wide staff and student reunion in about five years, so they would have an opportunity to get together again for sure. Melanie and Wally parted that night, with a big hug and birthday wishes from both of them. They shared a birthday, and were not sure if they would be able to call one another. Melanie went around and thanked all of them for coming and gave hugs to some of them, wishing them all well. For Melanie and the others, this had been the most fun they had had at a reunion!

Spring 1997

# THE BEER BOTTLE - PROJECTION TECHNIQUE

I am on the table, ¼ full and waiting to be finished. Three sips or maybe four. My label is Labatt Blue, and my alcohol level is not too high. My name or identity is unknown to me. I am a bottle of beer. Made by humans and being handled by them.

November 1998

# FRIENDS COMING & GOING CONTINUOUSLY

Some people bond and get along with everyone, some with very few. I get along with the few, or at least bond with the very few. Not having had siblings and not having many friends growing up, mostly due to my early speech problems and low self-esteem. I wanted to get along with Everyone. For me it is hard to approach someone and say, "Can I play" or "Can I join in?"

In grade school I was shunned out of many groups, being the odd one out in gym class, the last one chosen many times. In middle school, I started hanging out with and getting to know staff members and faculty at the schools I attended. Adults are far less judgmental and will often take the time to listen. My ability to bond to those select few seems to not be in my control and it is very interesting to look back years later.

Since then my self-esteem and confidence has increased by leaps and bounds, and my interest in self-discovery has been growing too. When I was 13, I thought I had minor psychological problems and that there was much that I didn't know. My mom rescued a small Yorkshire Terrier, named Mitsu from a main road near our home. She had been abused and neglected and had several homes since her original owner had passed away. We figured she was about six years old when we got her.

My heart reached out to this little one, as we seemed to have so much in common. We helped each other 'come out of the closet', both literally and figuratively, in terms of our fears and behavior and attitude towards life.

When mom and I moved out west, I had just turned 18 and thought I was ready to be on my own. I found out that there I needed to do grade 12 in order to get a high school diploma. Mom found me a great boarding school that was an all girl's school that had an equestrian program. It seemed to be the right thing to do. At this point in my life, where I had felt comfortable with who I was and was okay not having too many friends but a few true friends, I was put into a situation to start all over again. This was really trying for me and ended up making a few friends, however am not sure if they will be lifetime ones or not. My expectations socially were set so high that I underachieved in classes and became lazy, fearful and angry. I was angry at others and myself and fearful. Sometimes it felt justified other times it was not. I wonder what will happen in the next part of life?

Spring 1999

# The Caribbean Caper

Joan Marie is walking along a deserted beach in the Caribbean, when she hears some raised voices. She climbs up the cliff rocks and looks over, and sees a dinghy resting on the shore nearby. A small group of Hispanic men are being led along the seaside. They are blindfolded and appear to be poorly dressed. Out at sea, there is an ancient yet clean looking ship anchored.

The lead man opens a secret door in the rocks of the cliff and Joan sees them walking through this door and disappeared. In front of them is a pristine white mansion, built in colonial style with widow's peaks attached to the roof. Joan was curious as to what the men were doing. Knowing it was better she left the scene and decided she'd investigate that when she had time. Back at the hotel that she was staying at, she was expecting to see her husband, who worked as an Immigrations officer. There was going to be a dinner party that had been planned in the honour of her recent success in a Broadway play. Joan was a part time detective and part time actress. The hotel manager comes to Joan's room and informs her that her husband will be late for the party. The young man says to Joan that her husband was delayed at the airport and that it wasn't anything to worry about. He then asked if she would like him to escort her to the soiree in his place. Joan graciously accepts his offer. At the party, when the tea and coffee were being served, Joan's husband Bill walks in and whispers to Joan his apologies for missing most of the evening.

Pedro Garcia, the hotel manager seemed to be getting a little uncomfortable. Sitting beside Joan, he changed his position on the chair. Pedro wondered if he should say something about why he was there with Joan. Joan had been telling Bill about her adventure at the beach, and thought there may be a hot spring underneath the cliff. Joan and Bill leave a little early and go back to their room. Bill had been sporting a small cut on his right temple that needed tending. After completing this, Bill tells his wife to not divulge any more information of her travels that afternoon—to anyone.

The next morning, Joan decides to go back to the cove. She doesn't see any trace of the supposed explorers there. Joan touches most of the rock surfaces there, feeling for the thing that opened the compartmental door. Unbeknownst to her she was being watched. She walks down the passage way, once she finds the door trigger. Pedro sees her going into his private driveway. He decides to meet her part way and try to stop her. Pedro explains to her that his friends had taken the dinghy further up the shore to further their so called scientific exploration. Joan Marie becomes very suspicious and is almost convinced they were up to something- perhaps even something illegal. She then gets a feeling that she may be in danger. Her husband had decided to follow Joan, once he saw she had left. He had followed the footprints on the beach. He knew she was definitely in trouble. This was the same guy who had the airport delay him at the airport. Bill hurries on forward until he hears Pedro say that he is going to kill Joan, Pedro threatens Joan by grabbing her and telling her that he wants to show her his ancient torture chamber- that apparently was beneath this cliff. They continue to walk towards this underground mansion that Joan had seen or thought she saw the day before. Pedro stopped right before the gate to the mansion. Bill had followed them inside and stepped up and confronts Pedro. Bill updates Pedro, telling him that he knew who he really was and that he was involved in illegal trade.

When the semi-calm discussion escalates into a fight, Pedro rips out his 22 caliber gun and aims it at Joan. Bill lunges at Pedro, which causes Pedro to lose his grip on the gun. It lands on the ground near to where Joan was standing. She grabs it frantically and shoots Pedro in the abdomen. Pedro cried out in shock and pain and grasps his belly. Another shot is fired, this time by Bill. Writhing on the ground, Pedro calls Joan a bitch and soon after dies on the cavern's ground. Joan rushed over to Bill, who answers with a groan to the question of if he was okay. During the scuffle, he had been thrown down and he had hit his head again. This time on the left temple- and it was bruised. Joan whips Bills cell phone out of his uniform which Bill had been wearing. She calls the local security and an ambulance. He is brought to the hospital. A couple of days later, Bill had been released from the hospital with a clean bill of health. They decide to go on a second honeymoon together, the next time they sojourned. They were going to have the time of their lives!

Spring 1999

# LIFE PATHS:
# ITS ALTERNATIVES AND EXITS

W hile sitting in front of the squawk box, pondering the meaning and purpose of life, I began to think about the different people believe what their lives have been like in the past. That is, their past lives, for those who believe in them. People that have the ability to tap into the soul or spirit and ask questions have been known to tell certain few about their past lives. Other paranormal abilities and the ability to help people regress themselves are becoming part of the alternative health and wellness fields.

I wonder what would happen if people realized that they may be dealing with an issue from a past life, and it may be the cause of their angst in their current circumstances. Perhaps they could even learn to tap into that past life, and live part of it, so they could learn something and prevent it from becoming a problem in the current one. If a child with terminal cancer died before she had a chance to prepare, could she then after passing on, take that same form in spirit, and visit old friends and family and say goodbye? Some people say that they have seen or been to the other side, and have seen that white light and tunnel or gate.

In my beliefs, there is a heaven, or forever place where souls and guardians are. The soul is our essence that lives on throughout our different lives. It has the ability to carry memories and thoughts and perhaps a snippet of our personality. Souls must be something, because genuine psychics have tapped into something, whether it is a cloud of universal consciousness or souls. For many people the ability to tap into past lives, could very well be healing to some people and could explain what is occurring in their current lives.

Spring 1999

# McGill EcoMuseum Memories

On the West Island, located on the island of Montreal, Quebec there is a beautiful nature walk in the McGill Morgan Arboreteum. Only a thirty-five minute drive from downtown Montreal, it is very convenient to McGill students. The Arboreteum has a student rate for McGill students. If driving there one would exit at Morgan road, or at the Ste Anne De Bellevue exit and follow signs for the Arboreteum. Driving up the entrance gravel road, turning into their check in gate and continuing on to the parking lot. This nature walk through the woods is an educational opportunity as well, as they offer tours throughout the year for school groups and tourist groups. Guides take people through the forest and teach people about forestry, outdoor recreation and nature conservation and other topics.

Arboreteum literally means museum or collection of trees. They have many or all of the St. Lawrence Valley trees available to see and touch. The St Lawrence Valley extends from just south of Quebec City, to Ottawa. Because this park is completely outside, there are opportunities to experience the sound of nature, and to be part of it, as you learn about each part- living creatures of all sizes, plants, trees and humans. There was a movie partially filmed on location at the Morgan Arboretum about thirteen years ago. It was one of the King Arthur movies.... The Kids of The Round Table with Malcom McDowell as Merlin. There are a couple of scenes in the film that bring great memories of hiking and walking my dog in the Arboretum when I lived in Montreal.

Spring 2009

# SECTION 3:

# SHORT RESEARCH & ESSAYS

# THE PURPOSE OF EDUCATION

T he purpose of education in my opinion is to makes our lives miserable (in the words of some teenagers and youth) and partly to inform and educate us. One can become a better citizen through learning and develop self-discipline and valuable life skills. The most important part is the learning. We learn throughout our lives, not just at schools and learning centers. We learn about the history of the people we live with and those that surround us, we learn the language the people speak in the place one lives, and the language of those close by.

Students learn arithmetic and writing skills, and learn to read. In elementary school, students learn to read and write, and do basic math. In high school students learn more about the culture, history, of not only the people nearest them but worldwide cultures and languages. Geography and history and social sciences are taught throughout elementary and high school grades in many places but become very detailed as one progresses through the years. In mathematics you begin to learn additions and subtractions and by middle school, long division and multiplication tables are being used in geometry and beginning algebra. Calculators are used to calculate the solutions to more difficult problems. Education in schools is very important and those that pass through successfully will have the base for leading a very pleasant life.

Historically though it was thought and believed that children needed babysitting during the day when parents work outside of the home, and so schools were created. In our day and age when parents both work outside of the home, and the kids get home earlier than the parents, daycare services or after school activities or homework centers were created in some locations for these situations. Otherwise the children are labeled, 'latch-key kids' and they can be distinguished by having a chain or necklace with a key on it to their house. Or a friend or neighbor will be called upon to spend that two or three-hour time period with the children. Education systems were very different not that long ago. Mentoring programs and learning by being an apprentice and being told the story of the townspeople by word or written by scribes and passed down into generations that followed.

The other aspect of education is the learning of social graces, manners and learning about cultures other than one's own. This in turn teaches about religions, history and cultural meanings of many ethnicities in our world. Respect for others and interacting with others is something that is important throughout our lives. In all the centuries we have been living in North America, we still have not gotten the hang of the respect for other cultures, and many feuds, gang clashes and even community wars have begun because of ideology, lack of respect and lack of neutral and impartial education. We finally learn how to become better citizens and to get along with people that we meet. In conclusion, education is important for many ways and is carried out in more ways and not just in schools but we learn constantly throughout our lives.

Fall 1994

# *RAISE THE DRINKING AGE* GR 11 ENGLISH ARGUMENT ASSIGNMENT

The drinking age in Quebec and other places, should be raised to twenty-one years old because of irresponsible teens and young adults who are drinking and sometimes causing car accidents. When they drink and drive they are abusing the law and privileges bestowed upon those that learn to drive as a teenager.

Since the drinking age was lowered to eighteen years old, the driving age also changed, more young teens feel they deserve to be permitted to drive since it is legally allowed. Teenagers in high school, usually those in the higher grades, sometimes go out to bars using fake identification, and take part in night life in Montreal even though they are not legally permitted. They either use fake identification to get into clubs or a family member or good friend of legal age as a way in to these places. This is one reason the drinking age should be raised.

The second most important reason why the drinking age should be raised is that there are more accidents, usually car accidents, involving a drunken young person than there is a drunken older middle aged person. The percentage of people is very high, from ages sixteen to nineteen who get their licenses before graduating from high school. The percentage is equally high of accidents involving or caused by people between sixteen and twenty-six. For example, if a group of people are exiting the Peel Pub in Montreal's bar district, and are not sober not only is their safety in danger but other people's safety is too. This is especially the case if they decide they are sober enough to drive home. Designated driver programs are available as is late night public transit in Montreal and the surrounding areas.

If more people chose a designated driver who would choose to not drink at all or stay sober to ensure the safety of the other group members, fewer lives would get cut short because of car accidents and drinking and driving. With fewer accidents, the cost of Medicare would decrease as would the Canadian deficit. This would not only affect individuals but the whole country!

One of the most universal opinions about young people is that they are (or can be) delinquents and that many are not responsible. Young people tend to not take life seriously and play around a little thinking in their minds that they have all the time in the world. Young people (more so than older adults) play drinking games at parties and at university sororities. They will drink until they can no longer speak, which not only is dangerous for their health, but deadly if they decide to drive home.

These are the ones who cause most of the accidents on our roads today. The drinking age should be increased to protect our children and discourage the younger teens from partaking in illegal activities. These are a couple of reasons why I believe the drinking age should be raised to twenty-one.

Written 1996

# TREATMENT OF ANIMALS

I t is my firm belief that animals should be treated humanely and even appreciated for providing many humans with meat to eat or providing beauty care products that enable humans to look younger or better in certain circumstances.

In the past twenty years' people have been educated and informed about how many animals are treated before going to be killed for various reasons. One video entitled, *A Diet For A New America*, shows viewers how cows and pigs are treated with cruelty in many slaughter houses in farms. They showed hens and chickens kept in very small cages, with no room to turn around, their heads kept in the wire mesh bars, so they can eat and get fatter at a faster rate. Many times cows are kept chained in stalls and fed until they produce milk or until they are big enough to be killed for meat products that humans consume. I have even heard of hens being de-beaked and fed somehow until they lay eggs, and chickens are fed until they are big enough to eat.

It's not right to mistreat or misuse the animals we have grown accustomed to having supply most of our meals. Why for example, do we take some animals into our homes as pets and leave others to become endangered or even extinct? Pets that we bring home have sometimes been mistreated and end up emotionally unstable and physically wounded. For example, Greyhound dogs were used as race dogs, racing each other to give humans a reason to gamble their hard earned money, and entertainment for those who enjoyed it. Many of these dogs were sold to private homes when their racing careers are over, as they can barely walk in some cases and many need special medical care. Pitbulls received a bad reputation because they used to be used in dog fighting arenas in many regions. Pitbulls were sometimes so ferocious in the ring that they were not allowed to have a normal pet life, some were even euthanized because of their changed nature after fighting. This practice has been banned in many countries but is still done in some basement or garages illegally. We caused the image of the animals to be changed because humans were greedy, selfish and uncaring of the animals' feelings and mental status.

In the field of cosmetics, we test make up and skin products on animals such as lab rats and other small animals. In medicine we test vaccinations and treatments on animals too, many times it would require an animal with a similar genetic makeup so chimpanzees or other monkeys would be used. This is not right and although animals are still being used in some laboratories, there is legislation around this use and most of the time the animals are treated humanely.

I have heard people saying that dogs are not as smart as us humans, and that they think animals don't experience life as we do. I decided to do a short experiment with my dogs to see how they would react to my pretending to cry. I had two Yorkshire terriers and a poodle that I was pet sitting. The poodle, Brandy came up to me and sniffed the area around my eyes, then licked my cheek. The two yorkies came close to me and sniffed at my eyes and cheeks. I then lifted my face up so they could see that I was all right, they approached me again and licked me and appeared to smile. In my opinion and the interpretation of my results, the dogs wanted to see if I was okay, and wanted to see if I was crying. When the yorkie's saw that I did not have tears running down my face, they backed up and licked my cheek, as if to say they were glad I was okay. This told me that animals are aware of emotions, and cognizant of what crying and sadness is. It also tells me that they may believe that sadness can be relieved by love, or support. This concept is advanced in my opinion as grief processes count on the kindness and love of strangers and family alike. A simple smile or kind gesture can change the outcome of situations. If animals are aware of this and other similar emotional reactions, then they could not be labeled as stupid. Animals deserve a little more respect and the ones we kill for food should be treated humanely and with more respect as well.

Revised 2011, Originally written 1997

# WHY DO PEOPLE BULLY OTHERS?

Bullying can take many forms from physically hitting a person to insulting something one holds dear. The effects from bullying can last whether the victim is conscious of it or not for minutes or a lifetime. There are financial affects, physical affects, and psychological affects.

Firstly, the financial affects of being hit or battered either once or on a regular basis. In Canada we have health care where there are hospitals and emergency care available to most places with access to telephones. In the United States, health care is paid for by families who can afford it and Medicare for those who cannot.

If a child is battered and picked on continuously throughout school, they may require serious medical help. This treatment can be very costly over time. If counseling is needed that is sometimes not covered by Medicare or health plans and so people would need to pay for these non-life threatening services. However, if the circumstances warrant it, and suicide has been contemplated, most treatment centers will refer the family and client to emergency services in the counseling fields. Finances are often the least worry for parents of school children, however the expenses can become exorbitant.

Then there are the physical affects of actually being beaten or injured. Most likely to happen to boys or young tomboys in school, this can be very hard to get over. If the bullying is serious enough it may represent a necessary change in lifestyle, perhaps even being handicapped because of one mishap with a student's knife or gun. Most physical injuries will not last long given the time to heal. Physical abuse or spousal abuse can also be a form of bullying. As bullying can be a learned defense, anyone who was bullied and believes that its okay to bully someone they may be more likely to do it. Health care emergency services is vital in battered wives' situations or in school violence situations. Schools only have access to nurses most of the time and limited equipment and training to handle more than broken noses and minor injuries. Physical affects of bullying can be healed in most instances and should not be reason enough to worry about long term effects.

The most important thing that can cause worry to parents and family members is the emotional and psychological affects of bullying. In my personal experience bullying was not violent but a way for others to appear to be greater n rank and power at school and on playgrounds. I am scarred emotionally and psychologically by people who teased and taunted me because of my mild speech impediment. As mentioned above some extreme cases have ended in people taking their own lives as a solution to being bullied or exiled from those they love. These are very serious times and may be the last chance for people to realize what power they can have over others. Psychological and emotional traumas can last a lifetime.

Winter 2009

# THE BEGINNING OF THE WOMAN'S MOVEMENT

The Woman's Movement is an ongoing movement that started in the 1800's with equality and workers' conditions, one that started in Britain and eventually came across the pond, so to speak. The Feminist Movement sort of sprouted from the years following the Second World War. Simone de Beauvoir was "an intellectual and a novelist [coming from the ideological left]." Ms Beauvoir was a bisexual feminist in the second half of the twentieth century. So although more people may know of Margaret Thatcher, in my view it is Ms Beauvoir's life that resonates well with me and why I chose to write about her life.

"Ms Beauvoir was a French writer and philosopher and social theorist, Marxist and Maorist and a feminist (WIKI). She lived between 1908 and 1986 and was best known for "...her metaphysical novels, a detailed analysis of women's oppression and a foundational tract of contemporary feminism. She is also noted for her lifelong polyamorous relationship with Jean-Paul Sartre (Wiki)". Simone became a distinguished student and by the age of fifteen years she had decided to become a writer. Simone and her sister Helene were educated at the Institut Adeline Désir, where Simone graduated with distinction. "In 1929, while at the [University of Paris] Sorbonne, Beauvoir gave a presentation on Leibniz. This is when she met Jean Paul Sartre. While at the Sorbonne, Maheu gave Beauvoir her lifelong nickname, *Castor*, the French word for "beaver", given to her because of the animal's strong work ethic. (wiki)".

One of the written works Beauvoir had published was called, *La Deuxieme Sexe*. "Published in French, *The Second Sex* sets out a feminist existentialism which prescribes a moral revolution. As an existentialist, Beauvoir believed that existence precedes essence; hence one is not born a woman, but becomes one. (Wiki)" In the chapter "Woman: Myth and Reality" of *The Second Sex*, Beauvoir argued that men had made women the "Other" in society by putting a false aura of "mystery" around them. She argued that men used this as an excuse not to understand women or their problems and not to help them, and that this stereotyping was always done in societies by the group higher in the hierarchy to the group lower in the moral revolution. As an existentialist, Beauvoir believed that existence precedes essence; hence one is not born a woman, but becomes one. (Wiki)". In the in the current society views of who women are and what women want from relationships of all kinds are still based on traditional ways but as the demands of equality begin to amplify, the feminist musings of Simone de Beauvoir may start a new chapter of the Feminist Movement in North America. Therefore, Beauvoir has had more impact on today's society in general, whereas Thatcher impacted how businesses are run and how money is managed.

Winter 2009

(References were from Wikipedia's article on Margaret Thatcher and Simone De Beauvoir and from our history textbook).

# SCIENCE FAIR MEMORIES JOURNAL ENTRY

I n a private school in Notre Dame De Grace, which is a section of Montreal, Quebec there is a high school called Centennial Academy. I was a student there for most of my high school years. I enrolled there after grade 7, and completed my schooling to grade 11 at Centennial. There were about three hundred students at the time from grades seven to eleven. It is an independent school, non-denominational, it's a member of the Canadian Association of Independent Schools.

Nearing the end of my first year there in grade eight, my science teacher assigned science fair projects to the class. Each of us had to come up with a project to present to the class and the best of each class room would present at the school fair. If the project was innovative, well researched, presented nicely enough it could win the school fair and go on to the regional science fair.

It took me a long time to decide what project to do. Finally, I decided to research and combine the study of two avant garde subjects, Color and Light Therapy. It was one of my interests at the time and was something I was sure that the other students were not going to choose. Light therapy was being done in the United Kingdom at the White Lodge in Kent. My mother had studied it a little bit in her natural health courses she had completed the year before. Light was very scientific, and the new uses for lights and color as well may be very interesting to the teacher. It took me a while to read about light and color in the books I found at the library.

Since I had to present something as well as read my paper to the class, my mother suggested that I describe light therapy and how it is done. We decided that I would make a light box to show how light therapy and color therapy is combined and used for medical and spiritual healing. A trip to the local craft shop and hardware store did the trick. We bought some pink house insulation foam and a small halogen light and some different colored transparencies We also needed a piece of clear glass. We cut and assembled the foam into a box, and cut out a place for the glass to be held by the foam. We carved a hole for the light below where we put the glass with place for the electrical cord to pass through. On top of the glass, we cut out different pieces of light weight poster board (to divide each of the colored transparencies). The poster board made the walls of what could be the rooms where color therapy was practiced in Kent. In each of the spaces we placed and glued a colored transparency that had been cut to fit on the glass. That was how we created the model of what color therapy that was performed in special color coated rooms in Kent.

In my paper I not only described the therapy itself, but about the color spectrum and light spectrum. I described and told students that each color and sound has its own vibration, which in turn can affect a person's mood or health in one way or another.

As an anecdote, I also described the body's energy field and what a bumble bee sees when it sees a flower. I was really proud of myself for doing this project at that time.

A few days later I got my paper back from the teacher and was appalled by my grade, the teacher had given me a grade between 65 and 70 for both the presentation and the paper. I was not going to go on to the school level competition. I was really disappointed at the time. I was in grade eight in the year 1994.

Several years later, I had graduated grade eleven and had moved away from Montreal. I had thought I would never think of that project again. However, on a visit to the school just this past year, I spoke to the teacher again and decided to ask him if he remembered my project and asked his opinion on it. He did remember it! After almost 14 years, he remembered my light box and asked me if I was still interested in energies and alternative health. It felt really good to be remembered, and especially that he remembered this one project so many years later.

Thank you C. P!

Fall 2009

# RESEARCHING FAMILY HISTORY "HOW TO" ESSAY ASSIGNMENT

Researching family history can be a daunting endeavor especially if you do not know much about your ancestors. As better electronic resources emerge to assist with researching a family tree, the genealogical information is becoming more easily accessible to everyone. Though one still may need to access the archives for hard copies of articles, most archival information is uploaded from microfiche and is becoming viewable online. The relevant archives and the World Wide Web resources facilitate the process of creating a family tree. Utilizing these two resources makes creation of a family tree enjoyable. Family history is something that has intrigued me since I was a child. As the older generations pass away, it gets increasingly harder to learn about our genealogy through storytelling.

While talking with relatives and family friends may reveal part of the story, medical information or cultural heritage may not be remembered, as well some information may also be inaccurate or other details may be sketchy. Alternatively, one may just want to know about medical problems. For some people finding out their relationship to a celebrity or other famous person is reason enough to be enticed to do a genealogical search. It is good to know about one's family history for different reasons. World Wide Web resources such as Ancestry.com and Geneology.com are great places to start.

Another great resource is cemetery records, which can be accessed almost anywhere in the world via online search engines. The Jesus Christ of Latter Day Saints church website is also a very good resource. There are new computer programs to assist you in searching, for example the Family Tree Maker software is probably the most well-known at this time. Assuming you have any knowledge of your ancestors, you can find out quite a few more facts just by typing in their names and location into these search engines. If one has access to them, City or regional archives are great tools. Most places keep archives on census records, birth, death records and marriage records. There are librarians and research clerks at most city archives who are trained to help assist in searches such as these. As little as twenty-five years ago this task would have been overwhelming. With the creation of the Internet and all of its resources the genealogical research does not seem as daunting. There are many modern resources one can use to find one's ancestors including using the city archives and the World Wide Web. These will enable anyone to discover their unique family history.

Winter 2009

# WORDS OF WISDOM & QUOTES

For the quotes below, I am not sure what the original sources are, but they are sayings and well known comments that I have heard and received throughout my schooling years. The years are the dates that I had an impact from those words, or when I heard them for the first time.

Above All Else To Thine Own Self Be True
Words of Wisdom, 1992

Good people are good because they've come
to wisdom though wisdom.
Words of Wisdom, 2003

When it is dark about me,
I do not curse the darkness; I just light my candle.
Words of Wisdom, 2003

Love the people with whom fate brings you
together, and do so with all of your heart.
Words of Wisdom, 2005

What man (woman) can conceive and
believe - can certainly achieve.
Words of Wisdom, 2005

Words - A careless word may kindle strife -
A gracious word may smooth the way-
A brutal word may smite and kill - A loving word may
heal and bless - A timely word may light the day.
Words of wisdom, 2006

If You Could See Yourself As Others See You,
It Would From Many A Blunder Free You
Yearbook Inscription, 1963

At last I found a solution to all my problems....
But I've seemed to have forgotten all my problems!!!

I'm 2 cool 2 be forgotten, 2 people 2gether 4 ever!

It takes a lot of hard work and dedication
to be me so don't even try it!!!

Here are some lines to remember me by:
_____ _____ _____ _____

\*       \*       \*

Lots of Love, Sender
Finally - if you remember these sayings you were young in the 80s! -
Can't Touch This - Doesn't Matter If You Are Black or White -

Go Homeboy! Pump Up The Jam,
Dude! - Awesome - Radical - Cool!

Do not tell me of the people you associate with;
Let me observe it from your manners.

Courage is the price that life exacts for granting peace.
People who take time to be alone,
have depth, originality and quiet reserve.

The winds and waves are always on the side of the ablest navigators.

The Family That Prays Together, Stays Together!
Work may never hurt you but why take the chance?

# SECTION 5:

# LIFE LESSONS & BLOGS

Life is worth living, if I live life happy I will die happy and content.
If I live like unhappy and miserable, then I can affect many others.
If they live life being cruel to others, eventually they'll get it back.
Life Lesson #2, 1995

Love is such a powerful thing, treat it as thought you
are at war and two lovers are going to part. If it is meant
to be the two lovers will meet again after the war.
Life Lesson #3, 1995

Love, never go for it, let love come to you!
Life Lesson #7, 1996

This Moment will never come again - Spend each
moment of your life like you're going to die the next!
Life Lesson #9, 1997

Should you find a love so true, Gift wrap it an*d* save it -
Hold on to it and adore it, for as long as you live.
Life Lesson #10, 1997

When lovers must part do so amicably, for one never
knows where or when you will see them again.
Life Lesson #11, 2005

Without forgiveness life is governed by endless
cycles of resentment and retaliation.
Life Lesson #12, 2005

Patience is the companion of wisdom.
Life Lesson #13, 2006

# WHY DO PSYCHICS GIVE SOMEONE CONFLICTING INFORMATION?

This is a question that I have pondered for the recent months. I have spoken to many psychics in the past. The psychics that I tended to go back to were the ones that I could relate to in some way, ones that read what I know to be true, and not just the fears or holograms of what I was afraid of, or what seemed to be happening on the surface in my past relationships and career path.

I decided to research this a little bit more and found that just under 30% of practising psychics tend to tap into your current energy, or thought processes and repeat what they see or feel is currently going on. Time-frames cannot be predicted for the most part, because the universe is constantly changing, and time is not linear and there is the thing of free will. Mediums and psychics can tune into numbers or use tarot or playing cards to zoom in on a number or month or seasonal time reference, but things can change. When the asker knows something is true and accurate they could get readings to confirm what they already know on a higher level - and will develop the trust in themselves, and listen to what they know, and see and to what they are experiencing. Then if still in doubt or need assistance in interpreting their experiences they should ask for professional help. Yet it is important that in choosing a skills psychic/ medium that the problem starts. This can be very disconcerting and difficult. If you are getting conflicting answers it may be because you haven't decided which path to take. For example, a conflicting yes and no on a potential job at a specific company could mean there is something about the company that your subconscious doesn't trust.

For some oracle card readings, it is a question of will you meet someone this month or year? Those will be more specific and they are timing questions. Some readers choose not to interpret the time line that they may see, as it can be disconcerting to a rookie or to someone unaccustomed to doing so. Generally, the readers will pass along any information they will get from their source. For example, if they pull a SPRING card from the tarot, this indicates something will happen in terms of relationship in the spring if that was being asked.

So it is not always that the psychic is not delivering the correct information, but it could be that they are reading your doubts or your energies and not the person's you are enquiring about. Like you they can have 'off days' as well.

This blog is available to viewers with internet access. You may leave a comment or subscribe to my blog if you wish.

Published Spring 2009

# COLOR THERAPY & CHAKRAS

E very cell is light sensitive and also gives off its own light vibration. The cells of the skin act as light filters and allow light of all frequencies to pass to the tissues and cells through the body. Colour energy can be used to energize or balance the body's energy centres and can act as a catalyst for the body's own healing processes.

Colour therapy has no side effects and is perfectly safe whether being used for adults, children/babies or animals. Colour Therapy is a truly natural, holistic, non-invasive therapy. Colour Therapy aims to balance and enhance our body's energy centres/chakras by using the seven colours of the light spectrum, which can help to stimulate our body's own healing process. The body's chakra system and its colors in brief:

Violet:  Crown chakra, pineal gland and third eye, sometimes is seen as White light.

Indigo:  Forehead chakra, pituitary gland, lower brain and nervous system.

Blue:  Throat chakra, communication, metabolism, lungs.

Green:  Thymus gland, heart, circulatory system, immune and endocrine system.

Yellow:  Solar plexus, pancreas, spleen, stomach & nervous system, emotional sensitivity, personal power issues.

Orange: Sexual Organs, creativity, attitudes in relationships, reproduction.

Red:  Base chakra, spinal column, kidneys, adrenal gland.

My advice is to try a piece of clothing on that is primarily one of these colors, and see how it makes you feel. Notice any differences, whether negative or positive and adjust your clothes accordingly the following day. Meaning if a bright colored sweater makes you feel down, and the weather stays about the same, then change to a darker color and vice versa. You can get dressed as usual and then take note of the color of shirt you decided on wearing (for people who wear uniforms, etc of course- you can do that on your off time…) and note how that color makes you feel on that certain day.

Warmer Months bring lighter color clothes…help to make you feel airy, happy and hopeful. Enjoy your colors, play with them a bit and use them to understand yourself or others around you.

Published Summer 2009


THE END OF THIS WRITING - THANK YOU!

Dear Readers,

Thank you for taking the time to read my work. It means a lot to me and other writers that our words get out there. You too can have your voice heard, just like I have done. I welcome comments and questions by email, as well you can request a signed copy with personalization if you wish! Look for my next book - a children's book that will be coming by 2026 to bookshelves near you!

Sincerely,
Melanie Laurie Thiede

www.ingramcontent.com/pod-product-compliance
Lightning Source LLC
Chambersburg PA
CBHW051208120626
46547CB00013B/1251